THE YOUNG COTTAGER

THE

YOUNG

COTTAGER

AN AUTHENTIC NARRATIVE

BY

REV. LEGH RICHMOND

RECTOR OF TURVEY, BEDFORDSHIRE, ENGLAND

———

AND A VISIT TO THE ISLE OF WIGHT BY
REV. JAMES MILNOR, D.D.

CURIOSMITH
MINNEAPOLIS
2011

Published by Curiosmith.
P. O. Box 390293, Minneapolis, Minnesota, 55439.
Internet: curiosmith.com.
E-mail: shopkeeper@curiosmith.com.

Previously published by THE CHRISTIAN GUARDIAN in 1810.

ISBN 9781935626244

CONTENTS

PART I 7

PART II 20

PART III. 33

PART IV 44

PART V 61

PART VI 71

APPENDIX 85

PART I

WHEN a serious Christian turns his attention to the barren state of the wilderness through which he is travelling, frequently must he heave a sigh for the sins and sorrows of his fellow-mortals. The renewed heart thirsts with holy desire that the Paradise which was lost through Adam may be fully regained in Christ. But the overflowings of sin within and without, the contempt of sacred institutions, the carelessness of soul, the pride of unbelief, the eagerness of sensual appetite, the ambition for worldly greatness, and the deep-rooted enmity of the carnal heart against God: these things are as "the fiery serpents, and scorpions, and drought," which distress his soul, as he journeys through "that great and terrible wilderness."

Sometimes, like a solitary pilgrim, he weeps in secret places, and rivers of water run down his eyes, because men keep not the law of God.

Occasionally he meets with a few fellow-travellers whose spirit is congenial with his own, and with whom he can take "sweet counsel together." They comfort and strengthen each other by the way. Each can relate something of the mercies of his God, and how kindly they have been dealt with, as they travelled onwards. The dreariness of the path is thus beguiled, and now and then, for a while, happy experiences of the divine consolation cheer their souls; "the wilderness and the solitary place are glad for them; the desert rejoices and blossoms as the rose."

But even at the very time when the Christian is taught to feel the peace of God which passeth all understanding, to trust that he is personally interested in the blessings of salvation, and to believe that God will promote his own glory by glorifying the penitent sinner; yet sorrows will mingle with his comforts, and he will rejoice, not without trembling, when he reflects on the state of other men. The anxieties connected with earthly relations are all alive in his soul, and, through the operation of the Spirit of God, become sanctified principles and motives for action. As the husband and father of a family; as the neighbor of the poor, the ignorant, the wicked, and the wretched; above all, as the spiritual overseer of the flock, if such be his holy calling, the heart which has been taught to feel for its own case will abundantly feel for others.

But when he attempts to devise means in order to stem the torrent of iniquity, to instruct the ignorant, and to convert the sinner from the error of his way, he cannot help crying out, "Who is sufficient for these things?" Unbelief passes over the question, and trembles. But faith quickly revives the inquirer with the cheerful assurance that "our sufficiency is of God," and saith, "Commit thy way unto the Lord, and he shall bring it to pass."

When he is thus affectionately engaged for the good

of mankind, he will become seriously impressed with the necessity of early attentions to the young in particular. Many around him are grown gray-headed in sin, and give but little prospect of amendment. Many of the parents and heads of families are so eagerly busied in the profits, pleasures, and occupations of the world, that they heed not the warning voice of their instructor. Many of their elder children are launching out into life, headstrong, unruly, "earthly, sensual, devilish;" they likewise treat the wisdom of God as if it were foolishness. But, under these discouragements, we may often turn with hope to the very young, to the little ones of the flock, and endeavor to teach them to sing hosannas to the Son of David, before their minds are wholly absorbed in the world and its allurements. We may trust that a blessing shall attend such labors, if undertaken in faith and simplicity, and that some at least of our youthful disciples, like Josiah, while they are yet young, may begin to seek after the God of their fathers.

Such an employment, especially when blessed by any actual instances of real good produced, enlivens the mind with hope, and fills it with gratitude. We are thence led to trust that the next generation may become more fruitful unto God than the present, and the Church of Christ be replenished with many such as have been called into the vineyard "early in the morning." And should our endeavors for a length of time apparently fail of success, yet we ought not to despair. Early impressions and convictions of conscience have sometimes lain dormant for years, and at last revived into gracious existence and maturity. It was not said in vain, "Train up a child in the way he should go, and when he is old he will not depart from it."

What a gratifying occupation it is to an affectionate mind, even in a way of nature, to walk through the fields, and lead a little child by the hand, enjoying its infantine prattle, and striving to improve the time by some kind word of instruction! I wish that every Christian pilgrim in the way of grace, as he walks through the Lord's pastures, would try to lead at least one little child by the hand; and perhaps, whilst he is endeavoring to guide and preserve his young and feeble companion, the Lord will recompense him double for all his cares by comforting his own heart in the attempt. The experiment is worth the trial. It is supported by this recollection,—"The Lord will come with strong hand, and his arm shall rule for him; behold, his reward is with him, and his work before him. He shall feed his flock like a shepherd; he shall gather the lambs with his arm, and carry them in his bosom, and *shall gently lead those that are with young.*"

I shall plead no further apology for introducing to the notice of my readers a few particulars relative to a young female cottager, whose memory is particularly endeared to me from the circumstance of her being, so far as I can trace or discover, my first-born spiritual child in the ministry of the gospel. She was certainly the first, of whose conversion to God, under my own pastoral instruction, I can speak with precision and assurance.

Every parent of a family knows that there is a very interesting emotion of heart connected with the birth of his firstborn child. Energies and affections, to which the mind has hitherto been almost a stranger, begin to unfold themselves and expand into active existence when he first is hailed as a father. But may not the spiritual father be

allowed the possession and indulgence of a similar sensa-
tion in his connection with the children whom the Lord
gives him, as begotten through the ministry of the word
of life! If the first-born child in nature be received as a
new and acceptable blessing, how much more so the first-
born child in grace! I claim this privilege, and crave permission, in writing what follows, to erect a monumental
record, sacred to the memory of a dear little child, who, I
trust, will at the last day prove my crown of rejoicing.

Jane S—— was the daughter of poor parents, in the
village where it pleased God first to cast my lot in the
ministry. My acquaintance with her commenced when
she was twelve years of age by her weekly attendance at
my house amongst a number of children whom I invited
and regularly instructed every Saturday afternoon.

They used to read, repeat catechisms, psalms, hymns,
and portions of Scripture. I accustomed them also to pass
a kind of free conversational examination, according to
their age and ability, in those subjects by which I hoped
to see them made wise unto salvation.

On the summer evenings I frequently used to assemble
this little group out of doors in my garden, sitting under
the shade of some trees, which protected us from the heat
of the sun; from hence a scene appeared, which rendered
my occupation the more interesting. For adjoining the
spot where we sat, and only separated from us by a fence,
was the churchyard, surrounded with beautiful prospects
in every direction.

There lay the mortal remains of thousands, who, from
age to age, in their different generations, had been successively committed to the grave,—"earth to earth, ashes

I ASSEMBLED THIS LITTLE GROUP IN MY GARDEN.

to ashes, dust to dust." Here the once famed ancestors of the rich, and the less known forefathers of the poor lay mingling their dust together, and alike waiting the resurrection from the dead.

I had not far to look for subjects of warning and exhortation suitable to my little flock of lambs that I was feeding. I could point to the heaving sods that marked the different graves and separated them from each other, and tell my pupils that, young as they were, none of them were too young to die; and that probably more than half of the bodies which were buried there were those of little children. I hence took occasion to speak of the nature and value of a soul, and to ask them where they expected their souls to go when they departed hence and were no more seen on earth.

I told them who was "the resurrection and the life," and who alone could take away the sting of death. I used to remind them that the hour was "coming in the which all that are in the graves shall hear His voice, and shall come forth: they that have done good, unto the resurrection of life; and they that have done evil, unto the resurrection of damnation." I often availed myself of these opportunities to call to their recollection the more recent deaths of their own relatives that lay buried so near us. Some had lost a parent, others a brother or sister; some perhaps had lost all these, and were committed to the mercy of their neighbors as fatherless or motherless orphans. Such circumstances were occasionally useful to excite tender emotions, favorable to serious impressions.

Sometimes I sent the children to the various stones which stood at the head of the graves, and bid them learn the epitaphs inscribed upon them. I took pleasure in seeing the little ones thus dispersed in the churchyard, each committing to memory a few verses written in commemoration of the departed. They would soon accomplish the desired object, and eagerly return to me ambitious to repeat their task.

Thus my churchyard became a book of instruction, and every grave-stone a leaf of edification for my young disciples.

The church itself stood in the midst of the ground. It was a spacious antique structure. Within those very walls I first proclaimed the message of God to sinners. As these children surrounded me, I sometimes pointed to the church, spoke to them of the nature of public worship, the value of

MY CHURCHYARD BECAME A BOOK OF INSTRUCTION.

the Sabbath, the duty of regular attendance on its services, and urged their serious attention to the means of grace. I showed them the sad state of many countries, where neither churches nor Bibles were known, and the no less melancholy condition of multitudes at home, who sinfully neglect worship and slight the word of God. I thus tried to make them sensible of their own favors and privileges.

Neither was I at a loss for another class of objects around me from which I could draw useful instruction; for many of the beauties of created nature appeared in view.

Eastward of us extended a large river or lake of sea-water, chiefly formed by the tide, and nearly enclosed by land. Beyond this was a fine bay and road for ships, filled with vessels of every size, from the small sloop or cutter to the first-rate man-of-war. On the right hand of the haven rose a hill of peculiarly beautiful form and considerable height. Its verdure was very rich, and many hundred

sheep grazed upon its sides and summit. From the opposite shore of the same water a large sloping extent of bank
was diversified with fields, woods, hedges, and cottages.
At its extremity stood, close to the edge of the sea itself,
the remains of the tower of an ancient church, still preserved as a sea-mark. Far beyond the bay, a very distant
shore was observable, and land beyond it; trees, towns,
and other buildings appeared, more especially when
gilded by the reflected rays of the sun.

To the south-westward of the garden was another
down, covered also with flocks of sheep, and a portion of
it fringed with trees. At the foot of this hill lay the village,
a part of which gradually ascended to the rising ground
on which the church stood.

From the intermixture of houses with gardens, orchards,
and trees, it presented a very pleasing aspect. Several fields
adjoined the garden on the east and north, where a number of cattle were pasturing. My own little shrubberies and
flower-beds variegated the view, and recompensed my toil
in rearing them, as well by their beauty as their fragrance.

Had the sweet psalmist of Israel sat in this spot, he
would have glorified God the Creator by descanting on
these his handiworks. I cannot write psalms like David,
but I wish, in my own poor way, to praise the Lord for
his goodness, and to show forth his wonderful works to
the children of men. But had David been also surrounded
with a troop of young scholars in such a situation, he
would once more have said, "Out of the mouths of babes
and sucklings hast thou ordained strength."

I love to retrace these scenes; they are past, but the
recollection is sweet.

I love to retrace them, for they bring to my mind many former mercies, which ought not, for the Lord's sake, to be forgotten.

I love to retrace them, for they reassure me that, in the course of that private ministerial occupation, God was pleased to give me so valuable a fruit of my labors.

Little Jane used constantly to appear on these weekly seasons of instruction. I made no very particular observations concerning her during the first twelve months or more after her commencement of attendance. She was not then remarkable for any peculiar attainment. On the whole, I used to think her rather more slow of apprehension than most of her companions. She usually repeated her tasks correctly, but was seldom able to make answers to questions for which she was not previously prepared with replies—a kind of extempore examination, in which some of the children excelled. Her countenance was not engaging; her eye discovered no remarkable liveliness. She read tolerably well, took pains, and improved in it.

Mildness and quietness marked her general demeanor. She was very constant in her attendance on public worship at the church, as well as on my Saturday instruction at home. But, generally speaking, she was little noticed, except for her regular and orderly conduct. Had I then been asked of which of my young scholars I had formed the most favorable opinion, poor Jane might have been altogether omitted in the list.

How little do we oftentimes know what God is doing in other people's hearts! What poor calculators and judges we frequently prove till he opens our eyes! His thoughts are not our thoughts; neither our ways his ways.

Once, indeed, during the latter part of that year, I was struck with her ready attention to my wishes. I had, agreeably to the plan above mentioned, sent her into the churchyard to commit to memory an epitaph which I admired. On her return she told me that, in addition to what I desired, she had also learned another, which was inscribed on an adjoining stone, adding, that she thought it a very pretty one.

I thought so too, and perhaps my readers will be of the same opinion. Little Jane, though dead, yet shall speak. While I transcribe the lines, I can powerfully imagine that I hear her voice repeating them. The idea is exceedingly gratifying to me.

EPITAPH ON MRS. A. B.

Forgive, blest shade, the tributary tear
   That mourns thy exit from a world like this;
Forgive the wish that would have kept thee here,
   And stayed thy progress to the seats of bliss.

No more confined to grovelling scenes of night,
   No more a tenant pent in mortal clay;
Now should we rather hail thy glorious flight,
   And trace thy journey to the realms of day.

The above was her appointed task; and the other, which she voluntarily learned and spoke of with pleasure, is this:—

EPITAPH ON THE STONE ADJOINING.

It must be so—Our father Adam's fall,
   And disobedience, brought this lot on all.

All die in him—But, hopeless should we be,
Blest Revelation! were it not for thee.
Hail, glorious Gospel! heavenly light, whereby
We live with comfort, and with comfort die;
And view, beyond this gloomy scene the tomb,
A life of endless happiness to come.

I afterwards discovered that the sentiment expressed in the latter epitaph had much affected her, but at the period of this little incident I knew nothing of her mind; I had comparatively overlooked her. I have often been sorry for it since. Conscience seemed to rebuke me when I afterwards discovered what the Lord had been doing for her soul, as if I had neglected her, yet it was not done designedly. She was unknown to us all, except that, as I since found out, her regularity and abstinence from the sins and follies of her young equals in age and station brought upon her many taunts and jeers from others, which she bore very meekly; but at that time I knew it not.

I was young myself in the ministry, and younger in Christian experience. My parochial plans had not as yet assumed such a principle of practical order and inquiry as to make me acquainted with the character and conduct of each family and individual in my flock.

I was then quite a learner, and had much to learn.

And what am I now? A learner still; and if I have learned anything, it is this, that I have every day more and more yet to learn. Of this I am certain, that my young scholar soon became my teacher. I *first* saw what true religion could accomplish in witnessing her experience of it. The Lord once "called a little child unto him, and set him in the midst of his disciples" as an emblem and an illustration of his doctrine. But the Lord did more in the case of little Jane. He not only called *her* as a child to show, by a similitude, what conversion means, but he also called her by his grace to be a vessel of mercy, and a living witness of that almighty power and love by which her own heart was turned to God.

PART II

❧

THERE is no illustration of the nature and character of the Redeemer's kingdom on earth which is more grateful to contemplation, than that of the shepherd and his flock. Imagination has been accustomed, from our earliest childhood, to wander amongst the fabled retreats of the Arcadian shepherds. We have probably often delighted ourselves in our own native country, by witnessing the interesting occupation of the pastoral scene. The shepherd, tending his flock on the side of some spacious hill, or in the hollow of a sequestered valley; folding them at night, and guarding them against all danger; leading them from one pasture to another, or for refreshment to the cooling waters. These objects have met and gratified our eyes, as we travelled through the fields, and sought out creation's God, amidst creation's beauties. The poet and the painter have each lent their aid to cherish our delight in these imaginations. Many a descriptive verse has strengthened our attachment to the pastoral scene, and many a well-wrought picture has occasioned it to glow like a reality in our ideas.

But far more impressively than these causes can possibly affect, has the word of God endeared the subject to our hearts, and sanctified it to Christian experience. Who does not look back with love and veneration to those days of holy simplicity, when patriarchs of the church of God lived in tents and watched their flocks? With what a strength and beauty of allusion do the prophets refer to the intercourse between the shepherd and flock for an illustration of the Savior's kingdom on earth! The Psalmist rejoiced in the consideration that the Lord was his Shepherd, and that therefore he should not want. The Redeemer himself assumed this interesting title, and declared that "his sheep hear his voice, he knows them, and they follow him, and he gives unto them eternal life."

Perhaps at no previous moment was this comparison ever expressed so powerfully, as when his risen Lord gave the pastoral charge to the lately offending but now penitent disciple, saying, "Feed my sheep." Every principle of grace, mercy, and peace, met together on that occasion. Peter had thrice denied his Master: his Master now thrice asked him, "Lovest thou me?" Peter each time appealed to his own, or to his Lord's consciousness of what he felt within his heart. As often Jesus committed to his care the flock which he had purchased with his blood. And that none might be forgotten, he not only said, "Feed my sheep," but "Feed my lambs," also.

May every instructor of the young keep this injunction enforced on his conscience and affections,—I return to little Jane.

It was about fifteen months from the first period of her attendance on my Saturday school, when I missed her from her customary place. Two or three weeks had gone by, without my making any particular inquiry respecting her. I was at length informed that she was not well; but apprehending no peculiar cause for alarm, nearly two months passed away without any further mention of her name being made.

At length a poor old woman in the village, of whose religious disposition I had formed a good opinion, came and said to me, "Sir, have you not missed Jane S—— at your house on Saturday afternoons?"

"Yes," I replied, "I believe she is not well."

"Nor ever will be, I fear," said the woman.

"What! do you apprehend any danger in the case?"

"Sir, she is very poorly indeed, and I think is in a decline. She wants to see you, sir; but is afraid you would not come to see such a poor young child as she is."

"Not go where poverty and sickness may call me? How can she imagine so? At which house does she live?"

"Sir, it is a poor place, and she is ashamed to ask you to come there. Her near neighbors are noisy wicked people, and her own father and mother are strange folks. They all make game at poor Jenny because she reads her Bible so much."

"Do not tell me about poor places and wicked people: that is the very situation where a minister of the gospel is called to do the most good. I shall go to see her; you may let her know my intention."

"I will, sir; I go in most days to speak to her, and it does one's heart good to hear her talk."

"Indeed!" said I, "what does she talk about?"

"Talk about, poor thing! why, nothing but good things,

such as the Bible, and Jesus Christ, and life, and death, and her soul, and heaven, and hell, and your discourses, and the books you used to teach her, sir. Her father says he'll have no such godly things in his house; and her own mother scoffs at her, and says she supposes Jenny counts herself better than other folks. But she does not mind all that. She will read her books, and then talk so pretty to her mother, and beg that she would think about her soul."

"The Lord forgive me," thought I, "for not being more attentive to this poor child's case!" I seemed to feel the importance of infantine instruction more than ever I had done before, and felt a rising hope that this girl might prove a kind of first-fruits of my labors.

I now recollected her quiet, orderly, diligent attendance on our little weekly meetings; and her marked approbation of the epitaph, as related in my last paper, rushed into my thoughts. "I hope, I really hope," said I, "this dear child will prove a true child of God. And if so, what a mercy to her, and what a mercy for me!"

The next morning I went to see the child. Her dwelling was of the humblest kind. It stood against a high bank of earth, which formed a sort of garden behind it. It was so steep, that but little would grow in it; yet that little served to show not only, on the one hand, the poverty of its owners, but also to illustrate the happy truth, that even in the worst of circumstances the Lord does make a kind provision for the support of his creatures. The front aspect of the cottage was chiefly rendered pleasing by a honey-suckle, which luxuriantly climbed up the wall, enclosing the door, windows, and even the chimney, with its twining branches. As I entered the house-door, its flowers put forth

LITTLE JANE'S COTTAGE.

a very sweet and refreshing smell. Intent on the object of my visit, I at the same moment offered up silent prayer to God, and entertained a hope, that the welcome fragrance of the shrub might be illustrative of that all-prevailing intercession of a Redeemer, which I trusted was, in the case of this little child, as "a sweet-smelling savor" to her heavenly Father. The very flowers and leaves of the gar- den and field are emblematical of higher things, when grace teaches us to make them so.

Jane was in bed upstairs. I found no one in the house with her except the woman who had brought me the message on the evening before. The instant I looked on the girl, I perceived a very marked change in her countenance: it had acquired the consumptive hue, both white and red. A delicacy unknown to it before quite surprised me, owing to the alteration it produced in her look. She received me first with a very sweet smile, and then instantly burst into a flood of tears, just sobbing out,—

"I am so glad to see you, sir!"

"I am very much concerned at your being so ill, my child, and grieved that I was not sooner aware of your state. But I hope the Lord designs it for your good." Her eye, not her tongue, powerfully expressed, "I hope and think he does."

"Well, my poor child, since you can no longer come to see me, I will come and see you, and we will talk over the subjects which I have been used to explain to you."

"Indeed, sir, I shall be so glad!"

"That I believe she will," said the woman; "for she loves to talk of nothing so much as what she has heard you say in your sermons, and in the books you have given her."

"Are you really desirous, my dear child, to be a true Christian?"

"Oh, yes, yes, sir; I am sure I desire that above all things."

I was astonished and delighted at the earnestness and simplicity with which she spoke these words.

"Sir," added she, "I have been thinking, as I lay on my bed for many weeks past, how good you are to instruct us poor children; what must become of us without it!"

"I am truly glad to perceive that my instructions have not been lost upon you, and pray God that this your present sickness may be an instrument of blessing in his hands to prove, humble, and sanctify you. My dear child, you have a soul, an immortal soul to think of; you remember what I have often said to you about the value of a soul: 'What shall it profit a man, if he gain the whole world, and lose his own soul?"

"Yes, sir, I remember well you told us, that when our bodies are put into the grave, our souls will then go either to the good or the bad place."

"And to which of these places do you think that, as a sinner in the sight of God, you deserve to go?"

"To the bad one, sir."

"What! to everlasting destruction!"

"Yes, sir."

"Why so?"

"Because I am a great sinner."

"And must all great sinners go to hell?"

"They all deserve it; and I am sure I do."

"But is there no way of escape? Is there no way for a great sinner to be saved?"

"Yes, sir, Christ is the Savior."

"And whom does he save?"

"All believers."

"And do you believe in Christ yourself?"

"I do not know, sir; I wish I did; but I feel that I love him."

"What do you love him for?"

"Because he is good to poor children's souls like mine."

"What has he done for you?"

"He died for me, sir; and what could he do more?"

"And what do you hope to gain by his death?"

"A good place when I die, if I believe in him, and love him."

"Have you felt any uneasiness on account of your soul?"

"Oh, yes, sir, a great deal. When you used to talk to us children on Saturdays, I often felt as if I could hardly bear it, and wondered that others could seem so careless. I thought I was not fit to die. I thought of all the bad things I had ever done and said, and believed God must be very angry with me; for you often told us, that God would not be mocked; and that Christ said, if we were not converted, we could not go to heaven. Sometimes I thought I was so young it did not signify: and then, again, it seemed to me a great sin to think so; for I knew I was old enough to see what was right and what was wrong; and so God had a just right to be angry when I did wrong. Besides, I could see that my heart was not right; and how could such a heart be fit for heaven? Indeed, sir, I used to feel very uneasy."

"My dear Jenny, I wish I had known all this before. Why did you never tell me about it?"

"Sir, I durst not. Indeed, I could not well say what was the matter with me: and I thought you would look upon me as very bold, if I had spoke about myself to such a gentleman as you: yet I often wished that you knew what I felt and feared. Sometimes, as we went away from your house, I could not help crying; and then the other children laughed and jeered at me, and said I was going to be very good, they supposed, or at least to make people think so. Sometimes, sir, I fancied you did not think so well of me as of the rest, and that hurt me; yet I knew I deserved no particular favor, because I was the chief of sinners."

"My dear, what made St. Paul say he was chief of sinners? In what verse of the Bible do you find this expression, 'the chief of sinners;' can you repeat it?"

"'This is a faithful saying, and worthy of all acceptation, that Christ Jesus came into the world to save sinners;'—is not that right, sir?"

"Yes, my child, it is right; and I hope that the same conviction which St. Paul had at that moment has made you sensible of the same truth. Christ came into the world to save sinners: my dear child, remember now and for evermore, that Christ came into the world to save the chief of sinners."

"Sir, I am so glad he did. It makes me hope that he will save me, though I am a poor sinful girl. Sir, I am very ill, and I do not think I shall ever get well again. I want to go to Christ if I die."

"Go to Christ while you live, my dear child, and he will not cast you away when you die. He that said, 'Suffer little children to come unto me,' waits to be gracious to them, and forbids them not."

"What made you first think so seriously about the state of your soul?"

"Your talking about the graves in the churchyard, and telling us how many young children were buried there. I remember you said, one day, near twelve months ago, 'Children! where will you be a hundred years hence? Children! where do you think you shall go when you die? Children! if you were to die tonight, are you sure you should go to Christ and be happy?' Sir, I never shall forget your saying, 'Children,' three times together in that solemn way."

"Did you ever before that day feel any desire about your soul?"

"Yes, sir; I think I first had that desire almost as soon as you began to teach us on Saturday afternoons; but on that day I felt as I never did before. I shall never forget it. All the way as I went home, and all that night, these words were in my thoughts: 'Children! where do you think you shall go when you die?' I thought I must leave off all my bad ways, or where shall I go when I died?"

"And what effect did these thoughts produce in your mind?"

"Sir, I tried to live better, and I did leave off many bad ways; but the more I strove, the more difficult I found it, my heart seemed so hard: and then I could not tell any one my case."

"Could not you tell it to the Lord, who hears and answers prayers?"

"My prayers (here she blushed and sighed) are very poor at the best, and at that time I scarcely knew how to pray at all as I ought. But I did sometimes ask the Lord for a better heart."

There was a character in all this conversation which marked a truly sincere and enlightened state of mind. She spoke with all the simplicity of a child, and yet the seriousness of a Christian. I could scarcely persuade myself that she was the same girl I had been accustomed to see in past time. Her countenance was filled with interesting affections, and always spoke much more than her tongue could utter. At the same time she now possessed an ease and liberty in speaking, to which she had formerly been a stranger: nevertheless, she was modest, humble, and unassuming. Her readiness to converse was the result of spiritual anxiety, not childish forwardness. The marks of a Divine change were too prominent to be easily mistaken; and in this very child, I, for the first time, witnessed the evident testimonies of such a change. How encouraging, how profitable to my own soul!

"Sir," continued little Jane, "I had one day been thinking that I was neither fit to live nor die: for I could find no comfort in this world, and I was sure I deserved none in the other. On that day you sent me to learn the verse on Mrs. B——'s headstone, and then I read that on the one next to it."

"I very well remember it, Jenny; you came back, and repeated them both to me."

"There were two lines in it which made me think and meditate a great deal."

"Which were they?"

> "'Hail Glorious gospel! heavenly light, whereby
> We live with comfort, and with comfort die.'

I wished that glorious gospel was mine, that I might live and die with comfort; and it seemed as if I thought it would be so. I never felt so happy in all my life before. The words were often in my thoughts,—

> 'Live with comfort, and with comfort die.'

Glorious gospel, indeed! I thought."

"My dear child, what is the meaning of the word gospel?"

"Good news."

"Good news for whom?"

"For wicked sinners, sir."

"Who sends this good news for wicked sinners?"

"The Lord Almighty."

"And who brings this good news?"

"Sir, *you* brought it to *me*."

Here my soul melted in an instant, and I could not repress the tears which the emotion excited. The last answer was equally unexpected and affecting. I felt a father's tenderness and gratitude for a new and first-born child.

Jane wept likewise.

After a little pause she said,—

"O sir! I wish you would speak to my father, and mother, and little brother; for I am afraid they are going on very badly."

"How so?"

"Sir, they drink, and swear, and quarrel, and do not like what is good; and it does grieve me so, I cannot bear it. If I speak a word to them about it, they are very angry, and laugh, and bid me be quiet, and not set up for their teacher. Sir, I am ashamed to tell you this of them, but I hope it is not wrong; I mean it for their good."

"I wish your prayers and endeavors for their sake may be blessed; I will also do what I can."

I then prayed with the child, and promised to visit her constantly.

As I returned home, my heart was filled with thankfulness for what I had seen and heard. Little Jane appeared to be a first-fruits of my parochial and spiritual harvest. This thought greatly comforted and strengthened me in my ministerial prospects.

My partiality to the memory of little Jane will probably induce me to lay some further particulars before the reader.

PART III

❧

D IVINE grace educates the reasoning faculties of the soul, as well as the best affections of the heart; and happily consecrates them both to the glory of the Redeemer. Neither the disadvantages of poverty, nor the inexperience of childhood, are barriers able to resist the mighty influences of the Spirit of God, when "he goeth forth where he listeth." "God hath chosen the foolish things of this world to confound the wise; and God hath chosen the weak things of the world to confound the things which are mighty." The truth of this scriptural assertion was peculiarly evident in the case of my young parishioner.

Little Jane's illness was of a lingering nature. I often visited her. The soul of this young Christian was gradually, but effectually, preparing for heaven. I have seldom witnessed in any older person, under similar circumstances, stronger marks of earnest inquiry, continual seriousness, and holy affections. One morning, as I was walking through the church-yard, in my way to visit her, I stopped to look at the epitaph which had made such a deep impression on her mind. I was struck with the reflection of the important consequences which might result from a more frequent and judicious attention to the inscriptions placed in our burying-grounds, as memorials of the departed. The idea occurred to my thoughts, that as the two stone tables given by God to Moses were once a means of communicating to the Jews, from age to age, the revelation of God's will as concerning the law; so these funeral tables of stone may, under a better dispensation, bear a never-failing proclamation of God's will to sinners as revealed in the gospel of his grace, from generation to generation. I have often lamented, when indulging a contemplation among the graves, that some of the inscriptions were coarse and ridiculous; others, absurdly flattering; many, expressive of sentiments at variance with the true principles of the word of God; not a few, barren and unaccompanied with a single word of useful instruction to the reader. Thus a very important opportunity of conveying scriptural admonition is lost. I wish that every grave-stone might not only record the name of our deceased friends, but also proclaim the name of Jesus, as the only name given under heaven whereby men can be saved. Perhaps, if the ministers of religion were to interest themselves in this matter, and accustom their people to consult them as to the nature of the monumental inscriptions which they wish to introduce into churches and church-yards, a gradual improvement would take place in this respect. What is offensive, useless, or erroneous, would no longer find admittance, and a succession of valuable warning and consolation to the living would perpetuate the memory of the dead.

What can be more disgusting than the too common

spectacle of trifling licentious travellers, wandering about the church-yards of the different places through which they pass, in search of rude, ungrammatical, ill-spelt, and absurd verses among the grave-stones; and this for the gratification of their unholy scorn and ridicule! And yet how much is it to be deplored that such persons are seldom disappointed in finding many instances which too readily afford them the unfeeling satisfaction which they seek! I therefore offer this suggestion to my reverend brethren, that as no monument or stone can be placed in a church or church-yard without their express consent or approbation, whether one condition of that consent being granted, should not be a previous inspection and approval of every inscription which may be so placed within the precincts of the sanctuary?

The reader will pardon this digression, which evidently arose from the peculiar connection established in little Jane's history, between an epitaph inscribed on a gravestone, and the word of God inscribed on her heart. When I arrived at Jane's cottage, I found her in bed, reading Dr. Watts' Hymns for Children, in which she took great pleasure.

"What are you reading this morning, Jane?"

"Sir, I have been thinking very much about some verses in my little book. Here they are,—

'There is an hour when I must die,
   Nor do I know how soon 'twill come;
A thousand children young as I,
   Are called by death to hear their doom.

Let me improve the hours I have,

> Before the day of grace is fled;
> There's no repentance in the grave,
> Nor pardon offered to the dead.'

"Sir, I feel all that to be very true, and I am afraid I do not improve the hours I have, as I ought to do. I think I shall not live very long; and when I remember my sins, I say,—

> 'Lord, at thy feet ashamed I lie,
> Upward I dare not look;
> Pardon my sins before I die,
> And blot them from thy book.'

Do you think he will pardon me, sir?"

"My dear child, I have great hopes that he HAS pardoned you; that he has heard your prayers, and put you into the number of his true children already. You have had strong proofs of his mercy to your soul."

"Yes, sir, I have, and I wish to love and bless him for it. He is good, *very* good."

It had for some time past occurred to my mind that a course of *regulated* conversations on the first principles of religion would be very desirable from time to time, for this interesting child's sake: and I thought the Church Catechism would be the best groundwork for that purpose.

"Jenny," said I, "you can repeat the Catechism?"

"Yes, sir; but I think that has been one of my sins in the sight of God."

"What! repeating your Catechism?"

"Yes, sir, in such a way as I used to do it."

"How was that?"

"Very carelessly indeed. I never thought about the

meaning of the words, and that must be very wrong. Sir, the Catechism is full of good things; I wish I understood them better."

"Well, then, my child, we will talk a little about those good things which, as you truly say, are contained in the Catechism. Did you ever consider what it is to be a member of Christ, a child of God, and an inheritor of the kingdom of heaven?"

"I think, sir, I have lately considered it a good deal; and I want to be such, not only in name, but in deed and in truth. You once told me, sir, that 'as the branch is to the vine, and the stone to the building, and the limb to the body and the head, so is a true believer to the Lord Jesus Christ.' But how am I to know that I belong to Christ as a true *member*, which, you said one day in the church, means the same as a *limb* of the body, such as a leg or an arm?"

"Do you love Christ now in a way you never used to do before?"

"Yes, I think so indeed."

"Why do you love him?"

"Because he first loved me."

"How do you know that he first loved you?"

"Because he sent me instruction, and made me feel the sin of my heart, and taught me to pray for pardon, and love his ways; he sent you to teach me, sir, and to show me the way to be saved; and now I want to be saved in that way that he pleases. Sometimes I feel as if I loved all that he has said and done, so much, that I wish never to think about anything else. I know I did not use to feel so; and I think if he had not loved me first, my wicked heart would never have cared about him. I once loved anything better than religion, but now it is everything to me."

"Do you believe in your heart that Christ is able and willing to save the chief of sinners?"

"I do."

"And what are you?"

"A young, but a great sinner."

"Is it not of his mercy that you know and feel yourself to be a sinner?"

"Certainly; yes, it must be so."

"Do you earnestly desire to forsake all sin?"

"If I know myself, I do."

"Do you feel a spirit within you resisting sin, and making you hate it?"

"Yes, I hope so."

"Who gave you that spirit? Were you always so?"

"It must be Christ, who loved me, and gave himself for me. I was quite different once."

"Now, then, my dear Jane, does not all this show a connection between the Lord Jesus Christ and your soul? Does it not seem as if you lived, and moved, and had a spiritual being from him? Just as a limb is connected with your body, and so with your head, and thereby gets power to live and move through the flowing of the blood from the one to the other; so are you spiritually a limb or member of Christ, if you believe in him, and thus obtain, through faith, a power to love him, and live to his praise and glory. Do you understand me?"

"Yes, sir, I believe I do; and it is very comfortable to my thoughts to look up to Christ as a living Head, and to consider myself as the least and lowest of all his members."

"Now tell me what your thoughts are as to being a child of God."

"I am sure, sir, I do not deserve to be called his child."

"Can you tell me who *does* deserve it?"

"No one, sir."

"How, then, comes any one to be a child of God, when by nature we are children of wrath?"

"By God's grace, sir."

"What does grace mean?"

"Favor; free favor to sinners."

"Right; and what does God bestow upon the children of wrath, when he makes them children of grace?"

"A death unto sin, and a new birth unto righteousness; is it not, sir?"

"Yes, this is the fruit of Christ's redeeming love; and I hope *you* are a partaker of the blessing. The family of God is named after him, and he is the first-born of many brethren. What a mercy that Christ calls himself *'a Brother!'* My little girl, he is *your* Brother; and will not be ashamed to own you, and present you to his Father at the last day, as one that he has purchased with his blood."

"I wish I could love my Father and my Brother which are in heaven better than I do. Lord be merciful to me a sinner! I think, sir, if I am a child of God, I am often a rebellious one. He shows kindness to me beyond others, and yet I make a very poor return.

'Are these thy favors day by day,
    To me above the rest?
Then let me love thee more than they,
    And strive to serve thee best.'"

"That will be the best way to approve yourself a real child of God. Show your love and thankfulness to such a Father, who hath prepared for you an inheritance among the saints in light, and made you 'an inheritor of the kingdom of heaven, as well as a member of Christ, and a child of God.' Do you know what 'the kingdom of heaven' means?"

Just at that instant her mother entered the house below, and began to speak to a younger child in a passionate, scolding tone of voice, accompanied by some very offensive language; but quickly stopped on hearing us in conversation up stairs.

"Ah, my poor mother!" said the girl, "you would not have stopped so short, if Mr. —— had not been here. Sir, you hear how my mother swears; pray say something to her; she will not hear me."

I went towards the stair-head, and called to the woman; but ashamed at the thought of my having probably overheard her expressions, she suddenly left the house, and for that time escaped reproof.

"Sir," said little Jane, "I am so afraid, if I go to heaven I shall never see my poor mother there. I wish I may; but she does swear so, and keep such bad company. As I lie here a-bed, sir, for hours together, there is often so much wickedness, and noise, and quarrelling down below, that I do not know how to bear it. It comes very near, sir, when one's father and mother go on so. I want them all to turn to the Lord, and go to heaven.—Tell me now, sir, something about being an inheritor of the kingdom of heaven."

"You may remember, my child, what I have told you when explaining the Catechism in the church, that the 'kingdom of heaven' in the Scripture means the church of Christ upon earth, as well as the state of glory in heaven. The one is a preparation for the other. All true Christians are heirs of God, and joint-heirs with Christ, and shall inherit the glory and happiness of his kingdom, and live with Christ and be with him for ever. This is the free gift of God to his adopted children; and all that believe aright in Christ shall experience the truth of that promise, 'It is your Father's good pleasure to give you the kingdom.' You are a poor girl now, but I trust 'an entrance shall be ministered unto you abundantly into the everlasting kingdom of our Lord and Savior Jesus Christ.' You suffer now; but are you not willing to suffer for his sake, and to bear patiently those things to which he calls you?"

"Oh yes, very willing; I would not complain. It is all right."

"Then, my dear, you shall reign with him. Through much tribulation you may, perhaps, enter into the kingdom of God; but tribulation worketh patience; and patience, experience; and experience, hope. As a true 'member of Christ,' show yourself to be a dutiful 'child of God,' and your portion will be that of an inheritor of the kingdom of heaven. Faithful is He that hath promised. Commit thy way unto the Lord; trust also in him; and he shall bring it to pass."

"Thank you, sir, I do so love to hear of these things. And I think, sir, I should not love them so much if I had no part in them. Sir, there is one thing I want to ask you. It is a great thing, and I may be wrong—I am so young—and yet I hope I mean right—"

Here she hesitated and paused.

"What is it? Do not be fearful of mentioning it."

A tear rolled down her cheek—a slight blush colored her countenance. She lifted up her eyes to heaven for a moment, and then, fixing them on me with a solemn, affecting look, said,—

"May so young a poor child as I am be admitted to the Lord's Supper? I have for some time wished it, but dared not to mention it, for fear you should think it wrong."

"My dear Jenny, I have no doubt respecting it, and shall be very glad to converse with you on the subject, and hope that He who has given you the desire, will bless his own ordinance to your soul. Would you wish it now or tomorrow?"

"Tomorrow, if you please, sir;—will you come tomorrow and talk to me about it? and if you think it proper, I shall be thankful. I am growing faint now—I hope to be better when you come again."

I was much pleased with her proposal, and rejoiced in the prospect of seeing so young and sincere a Christian thus devote herself to the Lord, and receive the sacramental seal of a Savior's love to her soul.

Disease was making rapid inroads upon her constitution, and she was aware of it. But as the outward man decayed, she was strengthened with might, by God's Spirit in the inner man. She was evidently ripening fast for a better world.

I remember these things with affectionate pleasure; they revive my earlier associations, and I hope the recollection does me good. I wish them to do good to thee likewise, my reader; and therefore I write them down.

May the simplicity that is in Christ render

"The short and simple annals of the poor"

a mean of grace and blessing to thy soul! Out of the mouth of this babe and suckling may God ordain thee strength! If thou art willing, thou mayest perchance hear something further respecting her.

PART IV

⮕

I WAS so much affected with my last visit to little Jane, and particularly with her tender anxiety respecting the Lord's Supper, that it formed the chief subject of my thoughts for the remainder of the day.

I rode in the afternoon to a favorite spot, where I sometimes indulged in solitary meditation; where I wished to reflect on the interesting case of my little disciple.

It was a place well suited for such a purpose.

In the widely sweeping curve of a beautiful bay, there is a kind of chasm or opening in one of the lofty cliffs which bound it. This produces a very romantic and striking effect. The steep descending sides of this opening in the cliff are covered with trees, bushes, wild flowers, fern, wormwood, and many other herbs, here and there contrasted with bold masses of rock or brown earth.

In the higher part of one of those declivities two or three picturesque cottages are fixed, and seem half suspended in the air.

From the upper extremity of this great fissure, or opening in the cliff, a small stream of water enters by a

cascade, flows through the bottom, winding in a varied
course of about a quarter of a mile in length; and then
runs into the sea across a smooth expanse of firm, hard
sand, at the lower extremity of the chasm. At this point,
the sides of the woody banks are very lofty, and, to a spec-
tator from the bottom, exhibit a mixture of the grand and
beautiful not often exceeded.

Near the mouth of this opening was a little hollow
recess, or cave in the cliff, from whence, on one hand, I
could see the above-described romantic scene; on the
other, a long train of perpendicular cliffs, terminating in
a bold and wild-shaped promontory, which closed the bay
at one end, while a conspicuous white cliff stood directly
opposite, about four miles distant, at the further point of
the bay.

The shore, between the different cliffs and the edge
of the waves, was in some parts covered with stones and
shingle; in some, with firm sand; and in others, with
irregular heaps of little rocks fringed with sea-weed, and
ornamented with small yellow shells.

The cliffs themselves were diversified with strata of
various-colored earth, black, yellow, brown, and orange.
The effects of iron ore, producing very manifest changes of
hue, were everywhere seen in trickling drops and stream-
lets down the sides.

The huts in which the fishermen kept their baskets,
nets, boats, and other implements, occupied a few retired
spots on the shore.

The open sea, in full magnificence, occupied the cen-
ter of the prospect; bounded, indeed, in one small part,
by a very distant shore, on the rising ascent from which

the rays of the sun rendered visible a cathedral church,
with its towering spire, at near thirty miles' distance.
Everywhere else the sea beyond was limited only by the
sky.

A frigate was standing into the bay, not very far from
my recess; other vessels of every size, sailing in many
directions, varied the scene, and furnished matter for a
thousand sources of contemplation.

At my feet the little rivulet, gently rippling over peb-
bles, soon mingled with the sand, and was lost in the
waters of the mighty ocean. The murmuring of the waves,
as the tide ebbed or flowed, on the sand; their dashing
against some more distant rocks, which were covered fan-
tastically with sea-weed and shells; sea-birds floating in
the air aloft, or occasionally screaming from their holes in
the cliffs; the hum of human voices in the ships and boats,
borne along the water: all these sounds served to promote,
rather than interrupt, meditation. They were soothingly
blended together, and entered the ear in a kind of natural
harmony.

In the quiet enjoyment of a scene like this, the lover
of nature's beauties will easily find scope for spiritual
illustration.

Here I sat and mused over the interesting character
and circumstances of little Jane. Here I prayed that God
would effectually teach me those truths which I ought to
teach her.

When I thought of her youth, I blushed to think how
superior she was to what I well remember myself to have
been at the same age; nay, how far my superior at that
very time. I earnestly desired to catch something of the

spirit which appeared so lovely in her; for, simple, teach-
able, meek, humble yet earnest in her demeanor, she bore
living marks of heavenly teaching.

"The Lord," thought I, "has called this little child,
and set her in the midst of us, as a parable, a pattern,
an emblem. And he saith, 'Verily, except ye be converted,
and become as little children, ye shall not enter into the
kingdom of heaven.' Oh that I may be humble as this little
child!"

I was thus led into a deep self-examination, and was
severely exercised with fear and apprehension, whether
I was myself a real partaker of those divine influences
which I could so evidently discover in her. Sin appeared
to me just then to be more than ever "exceeding sinful."
Inward and inbred corruptions made me tremble. The
danger of self-deception in so great a matter alarmed me.
I was a teacher of others; but was I indeed spiritually
taught myself?

A spirit of anxious inquiry ran through every thought:
I looked at the manifold works of creation around me; I
perceived the greatest marks of regularity and order; but
within I felt confusion and disorder.

"The waves of the sea," thought I, "ebb and flow in
exact obedience to the law of their Creator. Thus far they
come, and no further—they retire again to their accustomed bounds; and so maintain a regulated succession of
effects.

"But, alas! the waves of passion and affection in the
human breast manifest more of the wild confusion of a
storm, than the orderly regularity of a tide. Grace only
can subdue them.

"What peaceful harmony subsists throughout all this lovely landscape! These majestic cliffs, some clothed with trees and shrubs; others bare and unadorned with herbage, yet variegated with many-colored earths; these are not only sublime and delightful to behold, but they are answering the end of their creation, and serve as a barrier to stop the progress of the waves.

"But how little peace and harmony can I comparatively see in my own heart! The landscape *within* is marred by dreary, barren wilds, and wants that engaging character which the various parts of this prospect before me so happily preserve. Sin, sin is the bane of mortality, and heaps confusion upon confusion, wherever it prevails.

"Yet, saith the voice of Promise, 'Sin shall not have dominion over you.' Oh, then, 'may I yield myself unto God, as one that am alive from the dead, and my members as instruments of righteousness unto God!' And thus may I become an able and willing minister of the New Testament!

"I wish I were like this little stream of water. It takes its first rise scarcely a mile off; yet it has done good even in that short course. It has passed by several cottages in its way, and afforded life and health to the inhabitants; it has watered their little gardens as it flows, and enriched the meadows near its banks. It has satisfied the thirst of the flocks that are feeding aloft on the hills, and perhaps refreshed the shepherd's boy who sits watching his master's sheep hard by. It then quietly finishes its current in this secluded dell, and, agreeably to the design of its Creator, quickly vanishes in the ocean.

"May *my* course be like unto thine, thou little rivulet! Though short be my span of life, yet may I be useful to my fellow-sinners as I travel onwards! Let me be a dispenser of spiritual support and health to many! Like this stream, may I prove 'the poor man's friend' by the way, and water the souls that thirst for the river of life, wherever I meet them! And if it please thee, O my God, let me in my latter end be like this brook. It calmly, though not quite silently, flows through this scene of peace and loveliness, just before it enters the sea. Let me thus gently close my days likewise; and may I not unusefully tell to others of the goodness and mercy of our Savior, till I arrive at the vast ocean of eternity!

"Thither," thought I, "little Jane is fast hastening. Short, but not useless, has been *her* course. I feel the great importance of it in my own soul at this moment. I view a work of mercy *there*, to which I do hope I am not quite a stranger in the experience of my own heart. The thought enlivens my spirit, and leads me to see that, great as is the power of sin the power of Jesus is greater; and, through grace, I *may* meet my dear young disciple, my child in the gospel, my sister in the faith, in a brighter, a better world hereafter."

There was something in the whole of this meditation which calmed and prepared my mind for my promised visit the next day. I looked forward to it with affectionate anxiety.

It was now time to return homewards. The sun was setting. The lengthened shadows of the cliffs, and of the hills towering again far above them, cast a brown but not unpleasing tint over the waters of the bay. Further on the beams of the sun still maintained their splendor. Some of the sails of the distant ships, enlivened by its rays, appeared like white spots in the blue horizon, and seemed to attract my notice, as if to claim at least the passing prayer, "God speed the mariners on their voyage."

I quitted my retreat in the cliff with some reluctance; but with a state of mind, as I hoped, solemnized by reflection, and animated to fresh exertion.

I walked up by a steep pathway, that winded through the trees and shrubs on the sides of one of the precipices. At every step the extent of prospect enlarged, and acquired a new and varying character, by being seen through the trees on each side. Climbing up a kind of rude, inartificial set of stone stairs in the bank, I passed by the singularly situated cottages which I had viewed from beneath; received and returned the evening salutation of the inhabitants, sitting at their doors, and just come home from labor; till I arrived at the top of the precipice, where I had left my horse tied to a gate.

Could *he* have enjoyed it, he had a noble prospect around him in every direction from this elevated point of view, where he had been stationed while I was on the shore below. But wherein he most probably failed I think his rider did not. The landscape, taken in connection with my recent train of thought about myself and little Jane, inspired devotion.

The sun was now set: the bright colors of the western clouds, faintly reflected from the south-eastern hills, that were unseen from my retreat in the cliff, or only perceived by their evening shadows on the sea, now added to the beauty of the prospect on the south and west. Every element contributed to the interesting effect of the scenery. The *earth* was diversified in shape and ornament. The *waters* of the ocean presented a noble feature in the landscape. The *air* was serene, or only ruffled by a refreshing breeze from the shore. And the sun's *fiery* beams, though departing for the night, still preserved such a portion of light and warmth as rendered all the rest delightful to an evening traveller. From this point the abyss, occasioned by the great fissure in the cliff, appeared grand and interesting. Trees hung over it on each side, projecting not only their branches, but many of their roots in wild and fantastic forms. Masses of earth had recently fallen from the upper to the lower parts of the precipice, carrying trees and plants down the steep descent. The character of the soil and the unceasing influence of the stream at the bottom, seemed to threaten further slips of the land from the summit. From hence the gentle murmur of the cascade at the head of the chine stole upon the ear without much interruption to the quietness of the scene. A fine rocky cliff, half buried in trees, stood erect on the land side about a mile distant, and seemed to vie with those on the shore in challenging the passenger's attention. In the distance stood a noble ash-tree, which, on a considerable height, majestically reigned as the patriarch of the grove near which it grew. Every object combined to please the eye and direct the traveller's heart to admire and love the Author and Creator of all that is beautiful to sense and edifying to the soul.

The next morning I went to Jane's cottage. On entering the door, the woman, who so frequently visited her, met me, and said:—

"Perhaps, sir, you will not wake her just yet; for she has dropped asleep, and she seldom gets much rest, poor girl!"

I went gently up stairs.

The child was in a half-sitting posture, leaning her head upon her right hand, with her Bible open before her. She had evidently fallen asleep while reading. Her countenance was beautifully composed and tranquil. A few tears had rolled down her cheek, and (probably unknown to her) dropped upon the pages of her book.

I looked around me for a moment. The room was outwardly comfortless and uninviting: the walls out of repair; the sloping roof somewhat shattered; the floor broken and uneven; no furniture but two tottering bedsteads, a three-legged stool, and an old oak chest; the window broken in many places, and mended with patches of paper. A little shelf against the wall, over the bedstead where Jane lay, served for her physic, her food, and her books.

"Yet *here*" I said to myself, "lies an heir of glory, waiting for a happy dismissal. Her earthly home is poor, indeed; but she has a house not made with hands, eternal in the heavens. She has little to attach her to this world; but what a weight of glory in the world to come! This mean, despised chamber is a palace in the eye of faith, for it contains one that is inheritor of a crown."

I approached without waking her, and observed that she had been reading the twenty-third chapter of St. Luke. The finger of her left hand lay upon the book, pointing to the words, as if she had been using it to guide her eye whilst she read.

I looked at the place, and was pleased at the apparently casual circumstance of her finger pointing at these words:—

"Lord, remember me when thou comest into thy kingdom."

"Is this casual or designed?" thought I. "Either way it is remarkable."

But in another moment I discovered that her finger was indeed an index to the thoughts of her heart.

She half awoke from her dozing state, but not sufficiently so to perceive that any person was present, and said in a kind of whisper:—

"Lord, remember me—remember me—remember—remember a poor child—Lord, remember me—"

She then suddenly started and perceived me, as she became fully awake. A faint blush overspread her cheeks for a moment, and then disappeared.

"Dame K——, how long have I been asleep?—Sir, I am very sorry—"

"And I am very glad to find you thus," I replied. "You may say with David, 'I laid me down and slept: I awaked, for the Lord sustained me.' What were you reading?"

"The history of the crucifying of Jesus, sir."

"How far had you read when you fell asleep?"

"To the prayer of the thief that was crucified with him; and when I came to that place I stopped, and thought what a mercy it would be if the Lord Jesus, should remember me likewise—and so I fell asleep; and I fancied in my dream that I saw Christ upon the cross; and I thought I said, 'Lord, remember me;' and I am sure he did not look angry upon me—and then I awoke."

All this seemed to be a sweet commentary on the text, and a most suitable forerunner of our intended sacramental service.

"Well, my dear child, I am come, as you wished me, to administer the sacrament of the body and blood of our blessed Savior to you; and I daresay neighbor K—— will be glad to join us."

"Talk to me a little about it first, sir, if you please."

"You remember what you have learned in your Catechism about it. Let us consider. A sacrament, you know, is 'an outward and visible sign of an inward and spiritual grace, given unto us, ordained by Christ himself, as a means whereby we receive the same, and a pledge to assure us thereof.' Now the Lord has ordained bread and wine in the holy supper, as the outward mark, which we behold with our eyes. It is a sign, a token, a seal of his love, grace, and blessing, which he promises to, and bestows on, all who receive it, rightly believing on his name and work. He in this manner preserves amongst us a 'continual remembrance of his death, and of the benefits which we receive thereby.'"

"What do you believe respecting the death of Christ, Jenny?"

"That because he died, sir, we live."

"What life do we live thereby?"

"The life of grace and mercy *now*, and the life of glory and happiness hereafter; is it not, sir?"

"Yes, assuredly: this is the fruit of the death of Christ, and thus he 'opened the kingdom of heaven to all believers.' As bread and wine strengthen and refresh your poor, weak, fainting body in this very sickness, so does the blessing of his body and blood strengthen and refresh the souls of all that repose their faith, hope, and affections on him who loved us and gave himself for us."

Tears ran down her cheeks as she said,—

"Oh, what a Savior! Oh, what a sinner! How kind! how good! And is this for me?"

"Fear not, dear child. He that has made you to love him thus, loves you too well to deny you. He will in no wise cast out any that come to him."

"Sir," said the girl, "I can never think about Jesus and his love to sinners, without wondering how it can be. I deserve nothing but his anger on account of my sins. Why then does he love me? My heart is evil. Why then does he love me? I continually forget all his goodness. Why then does he love me? I neither pray to him, nor thank him, nor do anything as I ought to do. Why then such love to me?"

"How plain it is that all is mercy from first to last! and that sweetens the blessing, my child. Are you not willing to give Christ all the honor of your salvation, and to take all the blame of your sins on your own self?"

"Yes, indeed, sir, I am. My hymn says,—

> 'Blest be the Lord, that sent his Son
> To take our flesh and blood;
> He for our lives gave up his own,
> To make our peace with God.

> 'He honored all his Father's laws,
> Which we have disobeyed;
> He bore our sins upon the cross,
> And our full ransom paid.'"

"I am glad you remember your hymns so well, Jenny."

"Sir, you don't know what pleasure they give me. I am very glad you gave me that little book of Hymns for Children."

A severe fit of coughing interrupted her speech for a while. The woman held her head. It was distressing to observe her struggle for breath, and almost, as it were, for life.

"Poor dear!" said the woman; "I wish I could help thee, and ease thy pains; but they will not last for ever."

"God helps me," said the girl, recovering her breath; "God helps me—he will carry me through. Sir, you look frightened. I am not afraid—this is nothing—I am better now. Thank you, dame, thank you. I am very troublesome; but the Lord will bless you for this and all your kindness to me: yes, sir, and yours too. Now talk to me again about the sacrament."

"What is required, Jenny, of them who come to the Lord's Supper? There are five things named in the Catechism; do you remember what is the first?"

She paused, and then said, with a solemn and intelligent look,—

"To examine themselves whether they repent them truly of their former sins."

"I hope and think that you know what this means, Jenny. The Lord has given you the spirit of repentance."

"No one knows, sir, what the thoughts of past sin have been to me. Yes, the Lord knows, and that is enough; and I hope he forgives me for Christ's sake. His blood cleanseth from all sin. Sir, I sometimes think of my sins till I tremble, and it makes me cry to think that I have offended such a God; and then he comforts me again with sweet thoughts about Christ."

"It is well, my child—be it so. The next thing mentioned in that article of your Catechism, what is it?"

"Steadfastly purposing to lead a new life."

"And what do you think of that?"

"My life, sir, will be a short one; and I wish it had been a better one. But from my heart I desire that it may be a *new* one for the time to come. I want to forsake all my evil ways and thoughts, and evil words, and evil companions; and to do what God bids me, and what you tell me is right, sir, and what I read of in my Bible. But I am afraid I do not, my heart is so full of sin. However, sir, I pray to God to help me. My days will be few; but I wish they may be spent to the glory of God."

"The blessing of the Lord be upon you, Jane; so that whether you live, you may live to the Lord; or whether you die, you may die unto the Lord; and that, living or dying, you may be the Lord's. What is the next thing mentioned?"

"To have a lively faith in God's mercy through Christ, sir."

"Do you believe that God is merciful to you in the pardon of your sins?"

"I do, sir," said the child earnestly.

"And if he pardons you, is it for your own sake, Jenny?"

"No, sir, no; it is for Christ's sake—for my Savior Jesus Christ's sake, and that only. Christ is all."

"Can you trust him?"

"Sir, I must not mistrust him; nor would I, if I might."

"Right, child; he is worthy of all your trust."

"And then, sir, I am to have a thankful remembrance of his death. I can never think of his dying, but I think also what a poor unworthy creature I am; and yet he is so good to me. I wish I *could* thank him—sir, I have been reading about his death—how could the people do as they did to him?—but it was all for our salvation. And the thief on the cross—that is beautiful. I hope he will remember me too, and that I shall always remember him and his death most thankfully."

"And lastly, Jenny, are you in charity with all men? Do you forgive all that have offended you? Do you bear ill-will in your heart to anybody?"

"Dear sir, no! how can I? If God is good to me, if he forgives me, how can I help forgiving others? There is not a person in all the world, I think, sir, that I do not wish well to for Christ's sake, and that from the bottom of my heart."

"How do you feel towards those bold, wanton, ill-tempered girls at the next door, who jeer and mock you so about your religion?"

"Sir, the worst thing I wish them is, that God may give them grace to repent; that he may change their hearts, and pardon all their wicked ways and words. May he forgive them, as I do with all my soul!"

She ceased—I wished to ask no more. My heart was full. "Can this be the religion of a child?" thought I. "O that we were all children like her!"

"Reach me that prayer-book, and the cup and plate. My dear friends, I will now, with God's blessing, partake with you in the holy communion of our Lord's body and blood."

The time was sweet and solemn. I went through the sacramental service.

The countenance and manner of the child evinced powerful feelings. Tears mingled with smiles—resignation brightened by hope—humility animated by faith—a child-like modesty adorned with the understanding of a riper age—gratitude, peace, devotion, patience—all these were visible. I thought I distinctly saw them all—and did *I* alone see them? Is it too much to say that other created beings, whom I could not behold with my natural eyes, were witnesses of the scene?

If ministering angels do ascend and descend with glad tidings between earth and heaven, I think they did so then.

When I had concluded the service, I said,—

"Now, my dear Jane, you are indeed become a sister in the Church of Christ. May his Spirit and blessing rest upon you, strengthen and refresh you!"

"My mercies are great, very great, sir; greater than I can express. I thank you for this favor—I thought I was too young—it seemed too much for me to think of; but I am now sure the Lord is good to me, and I hope I have done right."

"Yes, Jenny; and I trust you are both outwardly and inwardly *sealed* by the Holy Ghost to the day of redemption."

"Sir, I shall never forget this day."

"Neither, I think, shall I."

"Nor I," said the good old woman; "sure the Lord has been in the midst of us three today, while we have been gathered together in his name."

"Sir," said the child, "I wish you could speak to my mother when you come again. But she keeps out of your sight. I am so grieved about her soul, and I am afraid she cares nothing at all about it herself."

"I hope I shall have an opportunity the next time I come. Farewell, my child."

"Good-bye, sir; and I thank you for all your kindness to me."

"Surely," I thought within myself as I left the cottage, "this young bud of grace will bloom beauteously in paradise! The Lord transplant her thither in his own good time. Yet, if it be his will, may she live a little longer, that I may further profit by her conversation and example!"

Possibly, some who peruse these simple records of poor little Jane may wish the same. If it be so, we will visit her again before she departs hence and is no more seen.

PART V

JANE was hastening fast to her dissolution. She still, however, preserved sufficient strength to converse with much satisfaction to herself and those who visited her. Such as could truly estimate the value of her spiritual state of mind were but few; yet the most careless could not help being struck with her affectionate seriousness, her knowledge of the Scriptures, and her happy application of them to her own case.

"The holy spark divine,"

which regenerating grace had implanted in her life, had kindled a flame which warmed and animated the beholder. To *some*, I am persuaded, her example and conversation were made a blessing. Memory reflects with gratitude, whilst I write, on the profit and consolation which I individually derived from her society. Nor I alone. The last day will, if I err not, disclose further fruits, resulting from the love of God to this little child, and, through her, to others that saw her. And may not hope indulge the prospect, that this simple memorial of her history shall be as one arrow drawn from the quiver of the Almighty to reach the hearts of the young and the thoughtless? Direct its course, O my God! May the eye that reads, and the ear that hears, the record of little Jane, through the power of the Spirit of the Most High, each become the witness for the truth as it is in Jesus!

I remembered the tender solicitude of this dear child for her mother. I well knew what an awful contrast the dispositions and conduct of her parents exhibited, when compared with her own.

I resolved to avail myself of the first opportunity I could seize to speak to the mother in the child's presence. The woman had latterly avoided me, conscious of deserving, and fearful of receiving reproof. The road by which I usually approached the house lay, for some little distance, sufficiently in sight of its windows to enable the woman to retire out of the way before I arrived. There was, however, another path, through fields at the back of the village, which, owing to the situation of the ground, allowed of an approach unperceived, till a visitor reached the very cottage itself.

One morning, soon after the sacramental interview related in my last paper, I chose *this* road for my visit. It was preferable to me on every account. The distance was not quite half a mile from my house. The path was retired. I hereby avoided the noise and interruption which even a village street will sometimes present, to disturb the calmness of interesting meditation.

As I passed through the churchyard, and cast my eye on the memorable epitaph, "Soon," I thought within me, "will my poor little Jane mingle her moldering remains with this dust, and sleep with her fathers! Soon will the youthful tongue, which now lisps hosannas to the Son of David, and delights my heart with evidences of early piety and grace, be silent in the earth! Soon shall I be called to commit her 'body to the ground, earth to earth, ashes to ashes, dust to dust.' But oh, what a glorious change! Her spirit shall have then returned to God who gave it. Her soul will be joining the hallelujahs of paradise, while we sing her requiem at the grave. And her very dust shall here wait, in sure and certain hope of a joyful resurrection from the dead."

I went through the fields without meeting a single individual. I enjoyed the retirement of my solitary walk. Various surrounding objects contributed to excite useful meditation connected with the great subjects of time and eternity. Here and there a drooping flower reminded me of the fleeting nature of mortal life. Sometimes a shady spot taught me to look to Him who is a "shadow in the day-time from the heat, and for a place of refuge, and for a covert from storm and from rain." If a worm crept across my path, I saw an emblem of myself as I am *now*; and the winged insects, fluttering in the sunbeams, led me comparatively to reflect on what I hoped to be *hereafter*.

The capacious mansion of a rich neighbor appeared on the right hand as I walked; on my left were the cottages of the poor. The church spire pointing to heaven a little beyond, seemed to say to both the rich and the poor, "Set your affection on things above, not on things on the earth."

All these objects afforded me useful meditation; and all obtained an increased value as such, because they lay in my road to the house of little Jane.

I was now arrived at the stile nearly adjoining her dwelling. The upper window was open, and I soon distinguished the sound of voices—I was glad to hear that of the mother. I entered the house door unperceived by those above stairs, and sat down below, not wishing as yet to interrupt a conversation which quickly caught my ear.

"Mother! mother! I have not long to live. My time will be very short. But I must, indeed I must, say something for your sake, before I die. O mother! you have a soul—you have a soul; and what will become of it when you die? O my mother! I am so uneasy about your soul—"

"Oh, dear! I shall lose my child—she will die—and what shall I do when you are gone, my Jenny?" She sobbed aloud.

"Mother, think about your soul. Have you not neglected that?"

"Yes, I have been a wicked creature, and hated all that was good. What can I do?"

"Mother, you must pray to God to pardon you for Christ's sake. You must pray."

"Jenny, my child, I cannot pray: I never did pray in all my life. I am too wicked to pray."

"Mother, I have been wanting to speak to you a long time; but I was afraid to do it. You did not like me to say anything about religion, and I did not know how to begin. But indeed, mother, I must speak now, or it may be too late. I wish Mr. —— was here, for he could talk to you better than I can. But perhaps you will think of what I say, poor as it is, when I am dead. I am but a young child, and not fit to speak about such things to anybody. But, mother, you belong to me, and I cannot bear to think of your perishing for ever. My Lord and Savior has shown me my own sin and corruptions: he loved me, and gave himself for me: he died, and he rose again: I want to praise him for it for ever and ever. I hope I shall see him in heaven; but I want to see you there too, mother. Do, pray do, leave off swearing, and other bad ways: go to church, and hear our minister speak about Jesus Christ, and what he has done for wicked sinners. He wishes well to souls. He taught me the way, and he will teach you, mother. Why did you always go out of the house when he was coming? Do not be angry with me, mother; I only speak for your good. I was once as careless as you are about the things of God. But I have seen my error. I was in the broad road leading to destruction, like many other children in the parish; and the Lord saw me, and had mercy upon me."

"Yes, my child, you were always a good girl, and minded your book."

"No, mother, no; not always. I cared nothing about goodness, nor my Bible, till the minister came and sent for us, as you know, on Saturday afternoons. Don't you remember, mother, that at first you did not like me to go, and said you would have no such *godly, pious* doings about *your* house; and that I had better play about the streets and fields, than be laughed at and be made game of for pretending to be so good? Ah, mother, you did not know what I went for, and what God designed for me and my poor sinful soul! But, thank God, I did go, and there learned the way of salvation. Mother, I wish you had learned too."

As I listened to this affecting conversation, it appeared to me, from the tone and manner of the mother's voice, that she was more under the influence of temporary grief, on account of her child's extreme illness, than sincere sorrow from any real sense of her sins. I however hoped the best, and rejoiced to hear such weighty and important exhortation dropping from her daughter's lips. I felt that present circumstances rendered it far more valuable than my own could have been.

I have often, since that time, seen the wicked and careless much affected, while sitting by the dying bed of a near relative: I have witnessed their temporary acknowledgments of sin, and heard their professions of amendment. But, after a short season, all has passed away like the morning dew. The friend has been buried out of sight. The world and its cares, the flesh and its sins, have returned with new temptations, and the eloquence of iniquity has prevailed over the voice of truth. "The dog has returned to his vomit, and the sow to her wallowing in the mire."

On the other hand, how frequently have the deathbeds of true believers been blessed to the eye-witness of the triumphs of grace over sin, death, and hell! Often has the careless bystander received the first saving impression of divine truth, whilst the dying Christian has experienced and testified the supports of love and mercy in the trying hour. At such seasons, faith wields a bright and burning torch, which occasionally softens the hardest and warms the coldest heart. The expressions of that heavenly consolation and devout solicitude, which the Holy Spirit vouchsafes to some, thus become the happy means of grace and blessing for the conversion and edification of others.

"He that hath an ear, let him hear what the Spirit saith unto the churches!"

At this moment the house-door opened, and a younger

child, a brother of Jane's, came in. The mother asked from above who it was: the boy replied; and, without further inquiry, she remained in the chamber. I beckoned to the lad to sit down quietly; and thus it still remained unknown that I was below.

"Mother," continued Jane, "that is my brother, and will soon be your only remaining child. Do, pray, encourage him to follow good ways. Send him to Mr. ——, and he will be kind to him, as he has been to me. He is a wild boy, but I hope he will be brought to think about his soul in time. Those naughty, wicked boys teach him to swear and fight, and run after all manner of evil. Lord, help him to flee from the wrath to come!"

I made a sign to the boy to listen to what his sister said concerning him. He seemed to hear with attention, and a tear dropped down his cheek.

"Ay, Jenny, it is to be hoped he will, and that we shall all likewise."

"Mother, then you must flee to Christ. Nothing you can do will save you without that. You must repent and turn from sin: without the grace of God you cannot do it; but seek, and you shall find it. Do, for your own sake, and for my sake, and my little brother's sake."

The woman wept and sobbed without replying. I now thought it time to appear, went to the bottom of the stairs, and said, "May a friend come up?"

"Mercy on me!" said the mother, "there is Mr. ——."

"Come in, sir," said Jane; "I am very glad you are come *now*. Mother, set a chair."

The woman looked confused. Jane smiled as I entered, and welcomed me as usual.

"I hope I shall be forgiven, both by mother and daughter, for having remained so long below stairs, during the conversation which has just taken place. I came in the hope of finding you together, as I have had a wish for some time past to speak to you, Sarah, on the same subjects about which, I am happy to say, your daughter is so anxious. You have long neglected these things, and I wished to warn you of the danger of your state; but Jenny has said all I could desire, and I now solemnly ask you, whether you are not much affected by your poor child's faithful conversation? You ought to have been *her* teacher and instructor in the ways of righteousness, whereas she has now become *yours*. Happy, however, will it be for you if you are wise, and consider your latter end, and the things which belong to your peace, before they are hidden from your eyes! Look at your dying child, and think of your other and only remaining one, and say whether this sight does not call aloud upon you to hear and fear."

Jane's eyes were filled with tears whilst I spoke. The woman hung her head down, but betrayed some emotions of dislike at the plain dealing used towards her.

"My child, Jenny," said I, "how are you today?"

"Sir, I have been talking a good deal, and feel rather faint and weary, but my mind has been very easy and happy since I last saw you. I am quite willing to die, when the Lord sees fit. I have no wish to live except it be to see my friends in a better way before I depart. Sir, I used to be afraid to speak to them; but I feel today as if I could hold my peace no longer, and I must tell them what the Lord has done for my soul, and what I feel for theirs."

There was a firmness, I may say a dignity with which

this was uttered that surprised me. The character of the child seemed to be lost in that of the Christian; her natural timidity yielded to a holy assurance of manner resulting from her own inward consolations, mingled with spiritual desire for her mother's welfare. This produced a flush upon her otherwise pallid countenance, which in no small degree added to her interesting appearance. The Bible lay open before her as she sat up in the bed. With her right hand she enclosed her mother's.

"Mother, this book *you* cannot read; you should therefore go constantly to church, that you may hear it explained. It is God's book, and tells us the way to heaven; I hope you will learn and mind it; with God's blessing it may save your soul. Do think of that, mother, pray do. I am soon going to die. Give this Bible to my brother; and will you be so kind, sir, as to instruct him? Mother, remember what I say, and this gentleman is witness: there is no salvation for sinners like you and me but in the blood of Christ; he is able to save to the uttermost; he will save all that come to him; he waits to be gracious: cast yourself upon his mercy. I wish—I wish—I—I—I—"

She was quite overcome, and sank away in a kind of fainting fit.

Her mother observed, that she would now probably remain insensible for some time before she recovered.

I improved this interval in a serious address to the woman, and then prepared to take my departure, perceiving that Jane was too much exhausted for further conversation at that time.

As I was leaving the room, the child said faintly, "Come again soon, sir; my time is very short."

I returned home by the same retired road which I had before chosen. I silently meditated on the eminent proofs of piety and faith which were just afforded me in the scene I had witnessed.

Surely, I thought, this is an extraordinary child! What cannot grace accomplish? Is it possible to doubt after this, *who* is the alone Author and Finisher of salvation; or from *whom* cometh every good and perfect gift? How rich and free is the mercy of Jehovah! Hath not he "chosen the weak things of this world to confound the things which are mighty?" Let no flesh glory in his presence: but "he that glorieth, let him glory in the Lord."

PART VI

❧

THE truth and excellence of the religion of Jesus Christ appear to be remarkably established by the union of similarity with variety, in the effect which it produces on the hearts and lives of true believers. In the grand and essential features of Christian experience, the whole household of God possess an universal sameness of character, a family likeness, which distinguishes them from all the world besides: yet, in numerous particulars, there also exists a beautiful variety.

On the one hand, in the aged and the young, in the wise and the unlearned, in the rich and the poor; in those of stronger and weaker degrees of mental capacity, in more sanguine or more sedate dispositions; and in a multitude of otherwise varying circumstances, there is a striking conformity of principles and feeling to Christ, and to each other. Like the flowers of the field and the garden, they are "all rooted and grounded" in the soil of the same earth; they are warmed by the same sun, refreshed by the same air, and watered by the same dews. They each derive nourishment, growth, and increase from the same life-giving Source. As the flower puts forth its leaves and petals, adorns the place which it inhabits with its beauty, and possesses an internal system of qualities, whereby it is enabled to bring forth its seed or fruit in the appointed season; so does the Christian.

But, on the other hand, like the flowers also, some Christians may be said to grow on the mountain tops, some in valleys, some in the waters, and others in dry ground. Different colors, forms, and sizes, distinguish them from each other, and produce a diversity of character and appearance which affords a delightful variety, both for the purposes of use and beauty. Yet is that variety perfectly consistent with their essential unity of nature in the vegetable kingdom, to which they all equally belong.

In another particular they likewise resemble. They both die a natural death. The Lord ever preserves "a seed to serve him," from generation to generation; for as one disappears, another springs up to supply his place. But "it is appointed unto all men once to die."—Man "cometh forth like a flower and is cut down: he fleeth also as a shadow, and continueth not."—"All flesh is as grass, and all the glory of man as the flower of the grass. The grass withereth, and the flower thereof falleth away."

In the midst of such diversity of Christian characters there is much to love and admire. I have selected the case of little Jane, as one not undeserving of notice.

It is true, she was only a child—a very poor child—but a child saved by divine grace, enlightened with the purest knowledge, and adorned with unaffected holiness; she was a child, humble, meek, and lowly. She "found grace in the eyes of the Lord" while she was on earth; and, I doubt not, will be seen on his right hand at the last day. As such, there is preciousness in the character, which will account for my attempting once more to write concerning her, and describe her last moments before she went to her final rest.

At a very early hour on the morning of the following day, I was awoke by the arrival of a messenger, bringing an earnest request that I would immediately go to the child, as her end appeared to be just approaching.

It was not yet day when I left my house to obey the summons. The morning star shone conspicuously clear. The moon cast a mild light over the prospect, but gradually diminished in brightness as the eastern sky became enlightened. The birds were beginning their songs, and seemed ready to welcome the sun's approach. The dew plentifully covered the fields, and hung suspended in drops from the trees and hedges. A few early laborers appeared in the lanes, travelling towards the scene of their daily occupations.

All besides was still and calm. My mind, as I proceeded, was deeply exercised by thoughts concerning the affecting event which I expected soon to witness.

The rays of the morning star were not so beautiful in my sight, as the spiritual lustre of this young Christian's character. "Her night was far spent;" the morning of a "better day was at hand." The sun of eternal blessedness was ready to break upon her soul with rising glory. Like the moon, which I saw above me, this child's exemplary deportment had gently cast a useful light over the neighborhood where she dwelt. Like this moon she had for a season been permitted to shine amidst the surrounding darkness; and her rays were also reflected from a luminary, in whose native splendor her own would quickly be blended and lost.

The air was cool, but the breezes of the morning were refreshing, and seemed to foretell the approach of a beautiful day. Being accustomed, in my walks, to look for subjects of improving thought and association, I found them in every direction around me as I hastened onwards to the house where Jane lay, waiting for a dismissal from her earthly dwelling.

I felt that the twilight gravity of nature was, at that hour, peculiarly appropriate to the circumstances of the case; and the more so, because that twilight was significantly adorned with the brilliant sparklings of the star on one hand, and the clear, pale lustre of the waning moon on the other.

When I arrived at the house, I found no one below; I paused for a few minutes, and heard the girl's voice very faintly saying, "Do you think he will come? I should be so glad—so very glad to see him before I die."

I ascended the stairs—her father, mother, and brother, together with the elderly woman before spoken of, were in the chamber. Jane's countenance bore the marks of speedy dissolution. Yet, although death was manifest in the languid features, there was something more than ever interesting in the whole of her external aspect. The moment she saw me, a renewed vigor beamed in her eye; grateful affection sparkled in the dying face.

Although she had spoken just before I entered, yet for some time afterwards she was silent, but never took her eyes off me. There was animation in her look—there was more—something like a foretaste of heaven seemed to be felt, and gave an inexpressible character of spiritual beauty, even in death.

At length she said, "This is very kind, sir—I am going fast—I was afraid I should never see you again in this world."

I said, "My child, are you resigned to die?"

"Quite."

"Where is your hope?"

She lifted up her finger, pointed to heaven, and then directed the same downward to her own heart, saying successively as she did so, "Christ *there*, and Christ *here*."

These words, accompanied by the action, spoke her meaning more solemnly than can easily be conceived.

A momentary spasm took place. Looking towards her weeping mother, she said, "I am very cold—but it is no matter—it will soon be over—"

She closed her eyes for about a minute, and, on opening them again, said, "I wish, sir, when I am gone, you would tell the other children of the parish how good the Lord has been to me, a poor sinner—tell them, that they who seek him early will find him—tell them, that the ways of sin and ignorance are the ways to ruin and hell—and pray tell them, sir, from me, that Christ is indeed the Way, the Truth, and the Life—he will in no wise cast out any that come. Tell them that I, a poor girl—"

She was quite exhausted, and sunk for a while into a torpid state, from which, however, she recovered gradually, uttering these expressions: "Where am I?—I thought I was going—Lord, save me!"

"My dear child, you will soon be for ever in *His* arms

who is now guiding you by his rod and staff through the valley of the shadow of death."

"I believe so, indeed I do," said she; "I long to be with him!—Oh, how good, how great, how merciful!—Jesus, save me, help me through this last trial!"

She then gave one hand to her father, the other to her mother, and said, "God bless you, God bless you—seek the Lord—think of me when I am gone—it may be for your good—remember your souls—oh, for Christ's sake remember your souls—then all may be well—you cannot know what I have felt for both of you—Lord, pardon and save my dear father and mother!"

She then took hold of her brother's hand, saying, "Thomas, I beg you to leave off your bad ways—read the Bible—I give you mine—I have found it a precious book. Do you not remember our little brother, who died some years since?—he was praying to the last moment of his life. Learn to pray while you are in health, and you will find the comfort and power of it when you come to die; but, first of all, pray for a new heart—without it you will never see God in heaven—your present ways lead to misery and ruin— may the Lord turn your heart to love and follow him!"

To the other woman she said, "I thank you, Dame K——, for all your kindness since I have been ill—you have been a Christian friend to me, and I hope that the Lord will remember you for it, according to his rich mercy:— you and I have many a time talked together about death; and though I am the youngest, he calls me first to pass through it: but, blessed be his name, I am not terrified. I once thought I could never die without fear; but indeed I feel quite happy, now it is come; and so will you, if you trust him—he is the God both of the old and the young."

"Ah, my child!" said the woman, "I wish I was as fit to die as you are; but I fear that will never be—my sins have been many, very many."

"Christ's blood cleanseth from all sin," said the child.

At this moment, instead of growing weaker, through the fatigue of so much speaking, she seemed to gather fresh strength. She turned to me with a look of surprising earnestness and animation, saying,—

"You, sir, have been my best friend on earth—you have taught me the way to heaven, and I love and thank you for it—you have borne with my weakness and my ignorance—you have spoken to me of the love of Christ, and he has made me to feel it in my heart—I shall see him face to face—he will never leave me nor forsake me—he is the same, and changes not. Dear sir, God bless you!"

The child suddenly rose up, with an unexpected exertion, threw her livid, wasted arms around me, as I sat on the bedside, laid her head on my shoulder, and said distinctly, "God bless and reward you—give thanks for me to him—my soul is saved—Christ is everything to me! Sir, we shall meet in heaven, shall we not?—Oh yes, yes—then all will be peace—peace—peace—"

She sank back on the bed, and spoke no more—fetched a deep sigh—smiled—and died.

At this affecting moment, the rays of the morning sun darted into the room, and filled my imagination with the significant emblem of "the tender mercy of our God; whereby the dayspring from on high hath visited us, to give light to them that sit in darkness and in the shadow of death, to guide our feet into the way of peace."

It was a beam of light that seemed at once to describe the glorious change which her soul had now already experienced; and, at the same time, to shed the promised consolations of hope over the minds of those who witnessed her departure.

This was an incident obviously arising from a natural cause; but one which irresistibly connected itself with the spiritual circumstances of the case.

For some time I remained silently gazing on the breathless corpse, and could hardly persuade myself that Jane was indeed no longer there.

As I returned homeward, I found it difficult to repress the strong feelings of affection which such a scene had excited. Neither did I wish it. Religion, reason, and experience, rather bid us indulge, in due place and season, those tender emotions, which keep the heart alive to its most valuable sensibilities. To check them serves but to harden the mind, and close the avenues which lead to the sources of our best principles of action.

Jesus himself *wept* over the foreseen sorrows of Jerusalem. He *wept* also at the grave of his friend Lazarus. Such an example consecrates the tear of affection, while it teaches us, concerning them which are asleep, not to sorrow, as those which have no hope.

I soon fell into meditation on the mysterious subject of the flight of a soul from this world to that of departed spirits.

"Swifter than an arrow from the bow, or than the rays of light from the sun, has this child's spirit hastened, in obedience to its summons from God, to appear in his immediate presence. How solemn a truth is this for universal consideration! But, 'washed in the blood of the Lamb that was slain,' and happily made partaker of its purifying efficacy, she meets her welcome at the throne of God. She has nothing to fear from the frowns of divine justice. Sin, death, and hell, are all vanquished through the power of Him who hath made her more than conqueror. He will himself present her to his Father, as one of the purchased lambs of his flock—as one whom the Spirit of God 'has sealed unto the day of redemption.'

"What a change for her!—from that poor tattered chamber to the regions of paradise!—from a bed of straw to the bosom of Abraham!—from poverty, sickness, and pain, to eternal riches, health, and joy!—from the condition of a decayed, weary pilgrim in this valley of tears, to that of a happy traveller safely arrived at home, in the rest that remaineth to the people of God!

"I have lost a young disciple, endeared to me by a truly parental tie. Yet how can I complain of that as lost which God has found? Her willing and welcome voice no longer seeks or imparts instruction here. But it is far better employed. The angels, who rejoiced over her when her soul first turned to God, who watched the progress of her short pilgrimage, and who have now carried her triumphantly to the heavenly hills, have already taught her to join

'In holy song, their own immortal strains.'

Why then should I mourn? The whole prospect, as it concerns her, is filled with joy and immortality: 'Death is swallowed up in victory.'"

As I looked upon the dewdrops which rested on the grass and hung from the branches of the trees, I observed that the sun's rays first filled them with beautiful and varied colors; then dried them up, and they were seen no longer.

Thus it was with myself. The tears which I neither would nor could restrain, when I first began thus to reflect on the image of the dying chamber of little Jane, were speedily brightened by the vivid sunshine of hope and confidence. They then gradually yielded to the influence of that divine principle which shall finally wipe the tear from every eye, and banish all sorrow and sighing for evermore.

On the fourth day from thence, Jane was buried. I had never before committed a parishioner to the ground with similar affections. The attendants were not many, but I was glad to perceive among them some of the children who had been accustomed to receive my weekly private instruction along with her.

I wished that the scene might usefully impress their young hearts, and that God would bless it to their edification.

As I stood at the head of the grave, during the service, I connected past events, which had occurred in the church-yard, with the present. In this spot Jane first learned the value of that gospel which saved her soul. Not many yards from her own burial-place, was the epitaph which has already been described as the first means of affecting her mind with serious and solemn conviction. It seemed to stand at *this* moment as a peculiar witness for those truths which its lines proclaimed to every passing reader. Such an association of objects produced a powerful effect on my thoughts.

The evening was serene—nothing occurred to interrupt the quiet solemnity of the occasion.

"Peace" was the last word little Jane uttered while living; and peace seemed to be inscribed on the farewell scene of the grave where she was laid. A grateful remembrance of that peace revives in my own mind, as I write these memorials of it; and oh, may that peace which passeth all understanding be in its most perfect exercise, when I shall meet her again at the last day!

Attachment to the spot where this young Christian lay, induced me to plant a yew-tree close by the head of her grave, adjoining the eastern wall of the church. I designed it as an evergreen monument of one who was dear to memory. The young plant appeared healthy for a while, and promised by its outward vigor long to retain its station. But it withered soon afterwards, and, like the child whose grave it pointed out to notice, early faded away and died.

The yew-tree proved a frail and short-lived monument. But a more lasting one dwells in my own heart. And perhaps this narrative may be permitted to transmit her memory to other generations, when the hand and heart of the writer shall be cold in the dust.

Perchance some, into whose hands these pages may fall, will be led to cultivate their spiritual young plants with increased hopes of success, in so arduous an endeavor. May the tender blossoms reward their care, and bring forth early and acceptable fruit!

Some, who have perhaps been accustomed to undervalue the character of *very* youthful religion, may hereby see that the Lord of grace and glory is not limited in the exercise of his power by age or circumstance. It sometimes appears in the displays of God's love to sinners, as it does in the manifestations of his works in the heavens, that the *least* of the planets moves in the nearest course to the sun; and there enjoys the most powerful influence of his light, heat, and attraction.

The story of this Young Cottager involves a clear evidence of the freeness of the operations of divine grace on the heart of man; of the inseparable connection between true faith and holiness of disposition; and of the simplicity of character which a real love of Christ transfuses into the soul.

How many of the household of faith of every age,

"Alike unknown to fortune and to fame,"

have journeyed and are now travelling to their "city of habitation," through the paths of modest obscurity and almost unheeded piety! It is one of the most interesting employments of the Christian minister to search out these spiritual lilies of the valley, whose beauty and fragrance are nearly concealed in their shady retreats. To rear the flower, to assist in unfolding its excellences, and bring forth its fruit in due season, is a work that delightfully recompenses the toil of the cultivator.

While he is occupied in this grateful task of laboring in his heavenly Master's garden, some blight, some tempest, may chance to take away a favorite young blossom in a premature stage of its growth.

If such a case should befall him, he will then, perhaps, as I have often done, when standing in pensive recollection at little Jane's grave, make an application of these lines, which are inscribed on a gravestone erected in the same churchyard, and say—

"This lovely bud so young and fair,
  Called hence by early doom,
Just came to show how sweet a flower
  in paradise would bloom."

APPENDIX

Visit to the Graves of the Dairyman's Daughter and Young Cottager, July, 1823.

THE most interesting reflections, says a writer in the London Baptist Magazine for June, 1824, were suggested by a visit to the *Isle of Wight*,[1] in company with a long-respected Christian friend, who kindly solicited the writer to leave, for a few days, the cares and hurry of active life, for a scene so conducive to health and so exhilarating to the mind. It was scarcely possible to contemplate the works of God in that lovely island, without being reminded of that paradise which contributed to the happiness of our first parents in the days of their innocence, and which could not THEN fail to excite their holy admiration, and to elicit from them that glory to the Creator which corresponded with the powers with which they were endowed. We were effectually reminded, however, that the Isle of Wight was not the garden of Eden; for we beheld the memorials and the triumphs of death.

On entering the church-yards we saw, in *conspicuous* characters, the records of the generation that had passed

1 This beautiful island, which is about twenty-one miles long and thirteen broad, lies near the Southern shore of England.

away within our remembrance. Near *these* inscriptions we saw, in *fading* characters, a tribute of respect to the generation that passed away in the days of our fathers. We also saw stones and monuments covered with yellow and hoary lichen, and containing an account of the grand-fathers, and great grandfathers, and still more remote ancestors, till our attempts to make out the inscriptions ceased to be successful. On these occasions the reader may easily conceive that we were strongly impressed with the awful and extensive dominion of the king of terrors. Our object, however, was not so much to visit the tombs of the unknown among the dead, as to repair to those church-yards where we could find the sequestered spots devoted to those concerning whom we each could say, "Let me die the death of the righteous, and let my last end be like his!" In such researches we found the grave of "Little Jane," "the Young Cottager," in Brading church-yard, where the writer copied her epitaph.

On the following day, (July 16, 1823,) we visited the cottage where "the *Dairyman's Daughter*" had resided, and where she closed the days of her pilgrimage. Her mother, we were informed, did not long survive her affectionate daughter; and the aged Dairyman, we learned, had been dead a few years. The cottage is now occupied by her brother and his wife, both of whom we saw: and, among other interesting particulars, we were highly gratified with a sight of Elizabeth's Bible; on inspecting which, we saw not only her own hand-writing, but also that of a succession of ancestors for more than a century before her death.

Proceeding over the same ground as the funeral procession had done, we arrived at Arreton church-yard, where we found, without difficulty, the grave we sought. Indeed, every child seemed perfectly familiar with the spot.

The interesting Memoir, by Rev. T. S. Grimshawe, of the Author of the "Dairyman's Daughter," "the Young Cottager," and the "African Servant," substantiates each of those Tracts as a Narrative of facts which occurred under the author's ministry in the Isle of Wight, where he labored nearly eight years, when, in 1805, he was removed to Turvey, where he died, May, 1827, in the 56th year of his age, and the 30th of his ministry.

The Memoir contains a letter from Mr. John Higgins, a friend of Rev. Mr. Richmond, who, having obtained from him permission to examine the original letters of the Dairyman's Daughter, says, "It was not without pleasure and surprise I found, on the perusal of the originals, that they were in every respect as he had given them, with the exception of the bad spelling, the unnecessary use of capital letters, and a word which was here and there added or omitted to make the young woman's meaning more intelligible."

The Memoir also states that the Rev. Mr. Hughes, one of the Secretaries of the British and Foreign Bible Society, visited the spot where the Dairyman's Daughter formerly resided, and "interrogated her brother, whether the circumstances of the story were precisely the same as related in the Tract. To this he replied, there was *only one* fact that was misrepresented. Being asked, with some degree of anxiety, what the fact was, he observed, that Mr. Richmond had described *a vine*, trained by the side of the window, whereas it was *not a vine, but an apple-tree.*"

Nothing could be more satisfactory as to the essential

authenticity of the Narrative. The Memoir states (in 1828,) that 4,000,000 copies of this Tract were said then to have been circulated in nineteen different languages.

The reports of Tract Societies relate multitudes of instances in which this Tract has been blessed in the conversion of souls to God. Many such accounts were directly transmitted to the author, the last of which, received by him but 24 hours before his death, was that of a clergyman whose antipathy against Tract Societies had induced him to select the Dairyman's Daughter for the purpose of criticizing and exposing its defects. In the perusal of it he was so penetrated by the truths it contained, that the pen of criticism fell from his hand, and he was himself added as another trophy of Divine grace.

In 1822, Rev. Mr. Richmond visited the Isle of Wight, and the following is an extract of a pastoral letter, addressed, during his absence, to his congregation at Turvey: "I went one day to a part of my old parish where religion most prevailed, and sent word that I should be glad to shake hands with as many as would come down to the sea-shore, where I sat upon a rock. More than 500 men, women, and children came, and I gave each a Tract and a blessing. It was a scene full of deep and trying affections. I can never describe it, or think of it, without ardent feelings. We have put up grave-stones to Little Jane and the Dairyman's Daughter. Some hundreds attended, and the Tracts were distributed that respect those dear persons. It was a time of great feeling, and a tribute of much love was paid to the graves of the deceased. Some were there weeping with gratitude in having been brought to God through the reading of those very Tracts. The father and mother of Little Jane were at the grave while the stone was putting up. We then went to the house where she died, and the 'Young Cottager's Tract' was given to every one that came. It will be a sweet day of remembrance to me, for it took place on September 12. On that day, twenty-five years ago, I first received my own serious impressions through reading Mr. Wilberforce's book on Christianity, in my little study, at Brading; and Little Jane was the first fruits of my change of principles."

The Rev. Mr. Richmond received, in Scotland, numerous testimonies to the usefulness of his Tracts. On one occasion he distributed a copy of the 'Young Cottager' to each of sixty Sabbath School scholars, who encircled themselves around him. "Not an eye," he says, "was dry, and my own with difficulty allowed me to go through the simple and interesting ceremony. One girl, who was, two years since, converted by God's blessing on this Tract, as she approached me, was so affected, that she dropped on her knees and burst into tears."

[The following epitaph is on the gravestone of the Young Cottager.]

SACRED TO THE

MEMORY OF LITTLE JANE,

Who died Jan. 30, 1799, in the 15th year of her age.

> Ye who the power of God delight to trace,
> And mark with joy each monument of grace,
> Tread lightly o'er this grave, as ye explore
> "The short and simple annals of the poor."
> A child reposes underneath this sod,
> A child to memory dear, and dear to God.
> Rejoice, yet shed the sympathetic tear—
> Jane, the 'Young Cottager,' lies buried here.

JOURNAL OF A
VISIT TO THE ISLE OF WIGHT,
BY REV. JAMES MILNOR, D. D.
CHAIRMAN OF THE EXECUTIVE COMMITTEE
OF THE AMERICAN TRACT SOCIETY,
IN THE YEAR 1830.

WE were now approaching Brading, where the Rev. Legh Richmond commenced his ministry, were passing through the rich and delightful scenery which he so tastefully describes, and about to behold, and in some instances to press with our footsteps, those almost hallowed spots on which occurred events the remembrance of which he has perpetuated in those memorable Tracts, the "Young Cottager," the "African Servant," and the "Dairyman's Daughter." We had with us these invaluable Tracts, and employed ourselves in reading such parts of them especially as were calculated to direct our attention to the several places which he does not name, but describes with such fidelity to nature, that the observant traveler needs no other guide to point them out. I am glad that we can bear our testimony to the accuracy of his descriptions, because many have supposed them to be principally fanciful, and on this account much that adds greatly to the interest of his narrative, and is highly instructive in showing the Christian the religious feeling with which the works of the great Creator should be viewed, and the profitable use to which their contemplation may be applied, has been in many editions of them omitted. Though not so intended by the curtailers of these Tracts, the retrenchments, in my opinion, is an injustice to their lamented author, and an injury to the narratives themselves.

On arriving at Brading, we drove immediately to the church-yard where are interred the remains of little Jane. There were several children playing near the gate. I asked a fine-looking little girl if she could show us the grave of Jane, the Young Cottager. "O yes," she said, and advanced before us as our guide. After showing us the grave of Jane, and standing over it as long as we desired, in silent but affecting meditation, she told us she would show us the verses on Mr. and Mrs. Berry's tomb-stone, that Jane had got by heart, and repeated to Mr. Richmond. "Well, my dear," said I, "the reading of these verses helped Jane to become a good girl, and to die happy, did it not?" She answered, "Yes, Sir," as she did my next inquiry, whether she would not try to be as good a girl and die as happy as little Jane. The epitaphs which little Jane committed to memory, and especially the one on Mr. B.'s tomb-stone, which was probably the means, under God, of her first serious impressions, are both pious and affecting; and their influence on the mind of this youthful candidate for heaven may show the simple means the Holy Spirit often employs to accomplish the conversion of the soul to God.

We went from the grave-yard into the church, a very ancient structure, not less, the sexton assured us than eleven hundred years old. It has been enlarged since its first erection, and is remarkable for nothing, in its interior, but two singular tombs with wooden effigies of the deceased, several plainer but apparently very old monuments of stone, and a most helter-skelter inconvenient arrangement of the pews. Its location, however, is at once sequestered and convenient to the village, above which it is considerably elevated. The parsonage, a comfortable-looking abode, is immediately adjacent to the church-yard. From the church, the view of Brading Haven, the bay beyond, the elevated hill on the right, and the sloping bank upon the left, and the other scenery described by Mr. Richmond in the Young Cottager, as seen from this spot, are all just as there represented. On our way from Brading to Sandown-bay, the prospects were variegated and pleasing, and as we passed the fort, we emerged upon one of the grandest views of the ocean through the bay we had yet seen. Here was pointed to us the high down which Mr. Richmond describes in the African Servant, the perpendicular cliff in which it terminates, and the jutting rock under which he discovered and conversed so interestingly with his sable friend. Nothing could be more true to nature than the surrounding scenery as he describes it in that Tract.

We saw the cottage of the celebrated John Wilkes, in the garden of which are flourishing several rose-bushes, said to have been planted by his own hands. It is very near the water, but on an eminence so raised above it as to present an extensive sea-view. We then proceeded on to the village of Shanklin, consisting of a few neat cottages, and stopped at a residence bearing nothing of a tavern aspect, but affording us the refreshment we needed. After our lunch we walked down to what is called Shanklin Chine, a large romantic fissure or chasm in the cliff that fronts upon the sea. The descent to the beach is by an ordinary road, and then you return again through the chasm to Shanklin. No description extant of this singular spot is either so minutely accurate or so beautiful as that given by Mr. Richmond in the "Young Cottager," as one of his places of solitary religious meditation. We occupied the same "little hollow recess in the cliff" from which he surveyed and delineated the scenery around. We there read deliberately his graphic description of the various interesting objects that lay before him, and could discern no difference between it and the noble scene in actual view, except that a mist hid from us "the towering spire" of the Chichester Cathedral, that in these peaceful times we beheld no "frigate standing into the bay," and but few vessels of any description happened at that time to enliven the prospect. We lingered long upon and near the beach, and then proceeded up the chine, along the side of which the fishermen have formed a convenient footpath, with a resting-place or two on the way, where an interesting point of observation happened to offer. Several neat cottages with small gardens have been erected within the fissure, each of which, while sheltered from the weather by its lofty sides, enjoys an extensive prospect of the sea.

Returning to the village, we resumed our carriage, and passing by Shanklin church, a neat old edifice, we came to Bonchurch village, which is quietly seated in what is called the undercliff, a deep recess between a very lofty eminence or down on the inland side, and a high bank towards the sea. We got out of the carriage and proceeded along the bank, for the sake of the view which it presented of some excellent scenery not before disclosed. Below the village we threaded the way down a foot-path to the road, and got into out carriage, our course now lying up a valley between gently sloping but lofty hills on either side. Landscapes of peculiar beauty and variety, exhibiting numberless fields of grain nearly ripe for the harvest, herds of cattle and flocks of sheep, with here and there a company of hay-makers busily employed, presented themselves in ever-changing aspects as we ascended or descended the successive slopes of this delightful valley. We had long in sight, and at length passed at some distance, the splendid seat and extensive park and grounds of Lord Yarborough, called Appuldurcomb. Travelers have given rapturous descriptions of the interior and its rich collections of paintings and sculpture. Of these we shall probably never have a sight; but it was commended to our notice by circumstances of a very different kind. It was there that the sister of the Dairyman's Daughter died, whose funeral Mr. Richmond attended at the request of the latter; and where, on a visit about a week after, he had his first conversation with her whose religious experience, as narrated by that faithful minister, has had a more extensive influence in the world than ever attended any similar publication. He gives in the Dairyman's Daughter a correct account of the situation and appearance of Appuldurcomb, and of the adjacent scenery. We saw "the summit of the hill adjoining" the venerable mansion, to which he ascended after the visit referred to; the triangular pyramid of stone near which he sat down to meditate, and the magnificent surrounding prospect. In full view of this elevated spot we read his extended description, and turned southward, and southeastward, and northward, and westward, and admired, as he had done, the unequaled beauty of the scene. Certainly neither of us had ever read the descriptive part of the Dairyman's Daughter with the like interest and emotions. My feelings obliged me to resign the book to my companions, and under the various emotions the narrative and the scene excited, it was difficult for any of us to prosecute our reading; but with an intensity of interest we gazed upon the lovely prospect until it could be no longer seen.

We now approached Arreton, the village in the churchyard of which lie interred the mortal remains of Elizabeth Wallbridge, the sainted daughter of the Dairyman. About a mile from it we stopped before the cottage from which her soul ascended to its rest, and were kindly received by her surviving brother, a man now advanced in years, and still a resident in the mansion of his birth. He showed us Elizabeth's Bible, in which was simply written, "Elizabeth Wallbridge, daughter of Joseph and Elizabeth Wallbridge; born 1771–died 1801;" and took us up stairs into the room in which she expired. We added our names to a long list in a book kept by her brother for the purpose, and then took our leave; Mr. Wallbridge in a very respectful manner thanking us for our visit.

Our simplicity in finding satisfaction in such a visit, would be a fruitful subject of derision to men of the world; but if they will indulge our simplicity, and we can enjoy feelings such as these scenes excited, let them laugh, and we will delight in every thing calculated to cherish the memory of the pious dead.

On leaving the cottage, our path was the same as that over which moved the funeral procession of the Dairyman's Daughter, in the manner so affectingly described by Mr. Richmond. It lay through a narrow but excellent road, winding between high green hedges, and sometimes under an arch formed by the trees on either side; a lofty cultivated hill on the right, and a charming view of the luxuriant valley now and then breaking upon us to the left. As we read the account of the solemn passage of the mourning yet rejoicing relatives and friends of the deceased, we were ready almost to realize its actual vision, and hear the pious strains of melody as they then filled the air and ascended to the skies. Thus prepared, we reached Arreton church, and leaving our carriage to ascend the hill without us, we went to the grave of Elizabeth, read the beautiful lines which love of her character and the recollection of her triumphant death have caused to be inscribed on her simple monument, meditated for a while on her present glorious state, dropped a tear of sympathy, but not of sorrow, and silently retired.

From this to Newport, our destined resting-place, we could only talk on things connected with the scenes, and incidents, and reflections of the day; uniting in the sentiment, that Paris, with all its palaces, and gardens, and paintings, and statues, had afforded no such gratification to our eyes as the glorious works of God on which they had dwelt in this enchanting island; and none of its multiplied attractions such an inward feast as the mental associations of this day's travel had supplied.

NOTES

NOTES

NOTES

Printed in Great Britain
by Amazon